I Love You,
Dad

I Love You, Dad

A collection of poems
Edited by Susan Polis Schutz

Blue Mountain Press ™

Boulder, Colorado

Library of Congress Number: 83-071745
ISBN: 0-88396-197-0

The following works have previously appeared in Blue Mountain Arts publications:

"Thanks, Dad," by Miles M. Hutchinson. Copyright © Continental Publications, 1979. "Because of you, Dad," by Andrew Tawney. Copyright © Blue Mountain Arts, Inc., 1980. "You were always there," by Susan Polis Schutz. Copyright © Stephen Schutz and Susan Polis Schutz, 1982. "You may think that," by amanda pierce. Copyright © Blue Mountain Arts, Inc., 1982. "I love you, Dad" and "You know, there are so many things," by Andrew Tawney; "There will never be a day," by Laine Parsons; "Dad . . . ," by Lindsay Newman; and "As I pass through the days of my life," by Edmund O'Neill. Copyright © Blue Mountain Arts, Inc., 1983. All rights reserved.

Thanks to the Blue Mountain Arts creative staff.

ACKNOWLEDGMENTS appear on page 62.

Manufactured in the United States of America
First Printing: September, 1983

Blue Mountain Press INC.

P.O. Box 4549, Boulder, Colorado 80306

CONTENTS

"I love you, Dad"

What can you say
to someone who has
always been one of
the most essential parts of your world;
someone who took you by the hand
   when you were little
and helped to show the way . . .

What do you say to someone
who stood by to help you grow,
providing love, strength and support
so you could become the person
      you are today?

What can you say to let him know
that he's the best there is,
and that you hope you've inherited
   some of his wisdom and his strength?

What words would you say
   if you ever got the chance?

Maybe you just say
            "I love you, Dad . . ."

and hope he understands.

— Andrew Tawney

My Dad

Many men are strong, but very
few have been able to mix the
right amount of strength with a
proportionate amount of gentleness.
In doing so, you get a man you can
admire, respect, and look up to,
but also a man you can talk to
who will understand and listen.
All my life my father has given me a
feeling of security. No matter where
I go or what happens to me, I've always
known he's been back there watching
patiently should I need him. This
security has given me the strength to
stand on my own many times.

— James Bruce Joseph Sievers

Dad . . .

Do you remember when I was young . . .
   we used to laugh
      and play
   and you'd catch me and tickle me
      till the tears ran down my cheeks
I was so very small then,
   and you were so very big . . .
You took such care with me
   and protected me . . .
I may not have said it often enough,
   but somehow I thought
      you always knew . . .
         I love you, Dad.

— Debbie Avery

Dad, you're the kind of father every
    child longs for . . .
You've given me a firm foundation
    of faith
and taught me the importance of
    honesty in my life.
Because of that, I will always
    respect you.

Though our family has had hard times,
you've been a source of strength on
    which I can depend.
Yet, you've never been ashamed to
    reveal your weaknesses
or too proud to admit your mistakes.
That only reinforces my admiration
    for you. . .

But most important . . .
you've shown me the meaning of love,
always encouraging me to be the best
    that I can be.
Even when I fail or disappoint you,
your love never fails.

Thank you, Dad, for all you've done
    and all you've been to me.

— Susan Ellington

My Father . . .

Sometimes you used to let me
　　fall down,
just so I'd learn how to climb
　　back up again.
Sometimes you would try to keep
　　me from doing something
because you knew I'd be hurt,
but I'd do it and hurt myself
　　　　anyway.
Sometimes you were away
　　when I needed you,
but I always knew you'd come home
　　　　soon.
Sometimes you cried because
　　you were so proud of me,
and sometimes I cry
　　　　because I love you
　　　　　　so much.
　　　　Always, I'm thinking of you . . .

— Jean E. Attebury

You may think that
I haven't noticed all of
the thoughtful little things
    you do for me . . .
I know that I don't always
    say "thanks" . . .
But I have noticed,
and it's all those
    little things
and more . . .
that make me love you
    the way I do.

— amanda pierce

Thanks, Dad

Thanks for listening
Thanks for caring
Thanks for always helping
    in times of need
Thanks for sharing
Thanks, Dad
    for always being there

— Miles M. Hutchinson

Father

Kind and faithful, loyal and true,
Seeming, somehow, to know
Always the bravest and best thing to do,
Guiding my steps as I go,
Loving me tenderly all my life long,
Sharing each trouble I've had,
Patient and gentle, steadfast and strong
How dearly I love my Dad!

— Dorothy K. Fish

To My Father

When I was young
and learning to dream,
you were always there —
you listened . . . and encouraged
        me to follow
            my dreams . . .
You helped me to become
        all that I am.
Because you believed in me
        I learned to believe
in myself.
Thank you for everything.

— Linda DuPuy Moore

One father
is more than
a hundred schoolmasters.

— George Herbert

Only a dad, but he gives his all,
To smooth the way for his children small,
Doing with courage
    stern and grim
The deeds that his father did for him.
This is the line that for him
        I pen:
    Only a dad,
        but the best of men.

— Edgar A. Guest

For you, Father

You were always there
to help me
You were always there
to guide me
You were always there
to laugh with me
You were always there
to cry with me
But most important
You were always
there to love me
And believe me
I am always
here to love you

— Susan Polis Schutz

Thank you, Dad

It was the policy of my father
to make his children feel
that home was the happiest place
in the world;
and I value this home feeling
as one of the choicest gifts
a parent can bestow.

— Washington Irving

My Father . . .

I am always
asking much of you,
and like
life itself,
you always
give much.
May God bless you
     for all
          that you do
               for me.

— Kahlil Gibran

I want my father to be
just what he is . . .
a thoroughly human man,
   whom I admire,
         love and respect,
and who I hope will some day
hold the same sentiments toward me.

My greatest ambition
is to be
a "chip off the old block."

— A. C. Edgerton

To My Father

As I grow
I realize
that as I become
    more of "me" . . .
I become
    more like you.

And I can't think of
    any nicer thing to be.

— Stephen Richard Tapogna

When Parents Become Friends . . .

As a child, I sought your
    guidance and strength
to help me find happiness
    in life.
Now as an adult, I walk
    beside you
and find happiness in sharing
    your understanding,
        your love and
            your friendship.

— Edith Schaffer Lederberg

My Father

I have had happiness enough
to make life worth living . . .
and I feel that I owe all this
to you, my father, and that I can
in no way repay you except by telling
you over and over again
that I realize
every day more and more
what you have done for me
and are doing for me.

— Barrett Wendell

When you have the love
   of your family,
very few treasures in life
can surpass its value.
It is something that can never
   be taken away.
The love grows stronger
   as we grow older.
And as the love
      of our family has grown,
I have learned that the
   most wonderful way
      to thank you
   for all the love you gave . . .
      is to give it back.

— Maureen Peake

Because of you, Dad

Because of you I've come to experience an endearment to life and living, to love and to all that speaks of home.

For the affinity of father and child is a special union; a sacred and holy tie, a natural and earthly bond.

You have helped to raise and guide me through infancy and youth, from sapling to sturdy oak.

Together we are like a green and growing tree, nourished by the love of our immediate family and by our fathers' spirits before us.

Each year we grow stronger and yet more supple, able to bend without breaking and stand firm without faltering.

Our visible growth is easily perceived with each passage of time, but the union of father and child extends far beyond outward appearance and apparent change.

For in our quest for new heights — our ever-reaching branches against the sky — we have also grown deep and interwoven roots. . .

Together we share a common ground, and we take pride in our commitment.

Our love is a treasure that continues to increase — ever evolving to the eye; experienced ever deeper by the heart.

Surely, our companionship is a wondrous element of nature's design.

Out of the harvest of life, we will reap the rewards of family love and continuing contentment. A union such as ours will always weather the changing seasons.

My prayer is that I may pass along to my own children as much nourishment of the soul and as much fulfillment of the heart as you have given me.

I have realized a fine and full existence . . .
                              because of you, Dad.

— Andrew Tawney

Dad,
   why did it take me so long
      to see that . . .
. . . your "lectures" as I was growing up
         have unfolded as my appreciation of life;
. . . your taking us hiking on weekends
         has emerged as my love affair with nature;
. . . your talk of commitment
         has enabled me to be a loyal friend;
. . . your curiosity
         has freed me to become
         an inquirer about life;
. . . your dreams and idealism
         have helped me to have vision and purpose;
. . . your optimism
         has shown me the path
         to choosing happiness;
. . . your free expression of your love
         and concern for others
         has guided me to cherished relationships;
. . . your love of life
         has become my love of life.

What a beautiful legacy
      is mine
         because of you.

                              — Sue Mitchell

Dad . . .

When I was small
you looked so big . . .
I admired your strength
and how you could lift me up.
When I was small
I knew you were so talented
I admired your voice and
your touch and your abilities . . .
But when I was small
I overlooked so much in you.

Now that I'm grown,
I'm able to see all those
        other wonderful qualities, too.

— Kathy Ward

My Father and I

I am the image of your joy,
the smile of your happiness,
the longing of your goals.
You are my guide
to be as you are
    to feel
    to need
    to want.

You are a father
for whom
I honor my life
because you are
the image of my joy,
the smile of my happiness,
and the longing of my goals.
You have showered my life
with love
and given me
so much more
than I can ever return.

I hope that you're as proud of me
       as I am of you.

— jonivan

Father, it's your love
that safely guides me,
Always it's around me,
        night and day;
It shelters me,
        and soothes,
                but never chides me.

— Robert Bridges

I Admire My Dad

He doesn't tell me
how to live;

he lives,
and lets me
watch him do it.

— Clarence Budington Kelland

To My Father

From you, I have inherited strength
   on which to draw when I am weak;
determination
   on which to depend when I am
   discouraged;
courage
   on which to rely when I am afraid;
belief in myself
   on which to hope when I am in
   doubt.
Because you are my father,
   I have inherited a wealth
   of love.

— Andrea Marie Bertolini

My dear Father . . .
I feel so near to you now that
I do hope that nothing can ever
break the foundation of sincerity
that has been established beneath
our relations.

Never has anyone been kinder than you . . .
I want you to know that I appreciate it.

— Hart Crane

My dear papa, how shall I thank you?
It is easy to thank when
the gift of kindness is little.
It is difficult to thank
when it is great.

— John Ruskin

When I think of you,
I think of all the fulfillment
you bring into my life.
You radiate warmth and dependability,
inspiration and sincerity,
love and security.
Your quiet affirmations of love
erase all doubt and misbelief.
And above all else,
I think of your very soothing smiles
that generate such goodness and warmth.
I consider them a valuable necessity
of life.

Thank you for all your
beautiful contributions
to my happiness.

— Melissa Rolfe

My father is the saint of the family.
You work at something until you
exhaust yourself, so that you can be
good at it, and with it you try to
improve the lot of us . . .
You raise your children trying to
teach them decency and respect
for human life.

— Joan Baez

I think Daddy is the main reason
why I always had respect for myself . . .
I knew my Daddy loved me.

If I could . . . I would tell him
how much I love him.

— Loretta Lynn

When I was little, I asked you,
"What's it like to be grown up?"
Your wise answer was, "One day you'll see."
You knew it wouldn't be easy,
either to explain or do, yet you
patiently watched out for me as I grew.
Now the years have passed, and my place
is not that of a little child any longer.
I see now through eyes
which understand so much more;
especially the place you had
in helping this to be.

One thing that often comes to mind
is the way you were always there for me . . .
there to help, or guide, or correct;
and how I, in my naivete,
neglected to thank you.
Now that I have grown, I wish to
pause and try to make up for
those times by saying . . .
thank you.
Thank you for your love.
Thank you for being there
while I grew up.

— Cathy Highland

The family always came first with Dad, and by his example I learned that one can be deeply committed to both family and career without either suffering . . .

Some of my most precious memories of my father are those rare occasions when I had him all to myself. . . . But the times together as a family were special, too, from my earliest memories of him sitting through our childhood meals in the kitchen, making bird noises to amuse us and to keep our minds off the dreaded vegetables being shoveled into our mouths, to our most recent family evenings, playing cards, talking and laughing together.

Living up to an image and learning to accept ourselves and our parents for who we are is part of the process of growing up for all of us . . .

I always thought that growing up was something that happened to you; I didn't know it was something you have to work at, that it involved conscious decisions you have to make, sometimes with pain, sometimes with a great rending as you leave precious parts of your childhood behind.

Because of my father's values, I think that I was much less influenced by peer pressure than many young people. By his example, he taught me honesty, integrity and professionalism — to stand up for what you know is right for you.

. . . When people ask me what I value about my relationship with my parents, I name our communication, our respect, our playfulness, but too often I neglect to mention the one most valuable ingredient — our love.

— Kathy Cronkite

Father,
the world is a happier place
for having you here . . .

Your gift to life is a thoroughly
beautiful one . . . you simply present
yourself to those around you as one
full of kindness, full of sunshine,
bringing cheer and glad smiles of
welcome upon the faces of all who
know you. You walk quietly and
warmly through life, honored and
beloved by all who know you, and
wherever you have been, you leave
people happier and better for your
having been with them.

— Edward Chipman Guild

My father . . .

From your tolerance,
    I learned to accept.
From your encouragement,
    I learned to try.
From your support,
    I learned to succeed.
From your confidence,
    I learned to trust.
From your caring . . .
    I learned to love.

Thank you for giving my life
its beginning,
    — and so much of its meaning.

— Paula Finn

Father

If my mother is the heart,
he is the soul
of our family life.

— William Dean Howells

Rejoice
with your family
in the beautiful
land of life.

— Albert Einstein

Dad, I Love You

By watching your actions
    and contemplating your words,
I have grown to realize
    how truly blessed I am.
Your love has surrounded me in
    a realm of security and
       confidence,
often insulating me against
    the colder sides of life.
Yet, your protectiveness
    has respected my need for
       personal growth.
Attaining this delicate balance
    between providing guidance
       and granting freedom
is an achievement I will always
    appreciate and respect.
These thoughts seem hardly
    adequate
in expressing my gratitude for
    your lifelong commitment,
but I wanted to take this
    opportunity to remind you
how very proud I am of you.

— Barbara Lemke

The graduating class at
Yale University voted on this
question:
"What man in the world
do you most admire?"

And a majority answered:
"My father."

— William Lyon Phelps

My dear father . . .

When I was little
and a disappointment
threatened to crumble my world,
you'd hold me on your lap
and tell me things would
look brighter in the morning
   — and you were right.

When something seemed too difficult
and I was ready to give up,
you'd take me in your arms
and tell me
if I believed enough in myself
and kept trying,
I'd find I could do it after all
   — and you were right.

I admired you so much.
I thought I could never
outgrow my love for you
and that, as I got older,
you'd seem even more special to me
   — and I was right.

— Paula Finn

A special thought for you, Dad

You know, there are so many things
that I meant to say to you,
and somehow I never
quite got around to saying them.
Most of them have to do
with appreciation and thankfulness
   and happiness that you're here.
Looking back now,
it seems like sort of a shame
that such nice thoughts
that were meant for no one but you
never seemed to get beyond
   anyone but me. . .

I'm sorry I didn't share
    those things with you then . . .
but I know you understand.
You've always understood.
It's one of the nice ways you are . . .

I don't think I'll ever be
able to make up for all that lost time,
but maybe I can turn over a new leaf . . .
one that will allow me
to let you know
    and to remind you from time to time . . .
        that I love you a lot.

— Andrew Tawney

Dad . . .

When I was just a child,
I used to think that you knew
   all there was to know.
I could come to you with any
question back then, like . . .
      why is the world round, or
      where do trees come from, or
      what makes an airplane go . . .
and you always had the answer.

Well, I guess my questions have
gotten a little harder since then,
      but the nice thing is . . .
I know I can still come to you
      with them.
And even if you don't always have
      the answer,
I find as much satisfaction talking
      things over with you today
as I did when I was just a child.

— Lindsay Newman

Dad, There Will Never Be . . .

There will never be a day
when I won't smile a quiet smile
and say an unspoken thanks . . .
           just for you

There will never come a time
when I won't think of
all the special things about you —
     you with the gentle touch
     and the warming grin
     and the kindest eyes
          I've ever known . . .

For there will never be
          a day in my life
          that you will not be a part of.

                    — Laine Parsons

Dear Dad,

I remember when I was younger — I used to jump into your lap or run to your arms for safety. It seemed only natural to tell you of my hurt or fear. You protected me and made it better. Now I am older, and hurts and fears seem more complex. Safety is hard to chance upon. But often, I find I am consoled by thoughts of how you have comforted me in moments passed, and sometimes I still wish for the warmth of your arms. I know that people change, but I hope I never grow so much that I'm too big to find solace in a hug from you, or too distant to sense when you have the same need . . .

— Rowland R. Hoskins, Jr.

My Father

As I pass through the days of my life,
I carry with me the gifts you have
always shared so generously . . .
for you've given me
a better understanding of the world
and my place in it
with the gifts of your wisdom
and patience . . .
and you've made my smile brighter
with the gift of your laughter . . .
you've made some hard times
a lighter burden for me to bear
with the strength of your inner spirit . . .
and by always being there
when the sunshine returned . . .
Forever I'm grateful
for all the gifts you've shared with me.

— Edmund O'Neill

ACKNOWLEDGMENTS

We gratefully acknowledge the permission granted by the following authors, publishers and authors' representatives to reprint poems and excerpts from their publications:

Skybird Publishing Company for "My Dad," by James Bruce Joseph Sievers. Copyright © Skybird Publishing Company, 1976. All rights reserved. Reprinted by permission.

Debbie Avery for "Dad . . . ," by Debbie Avery. Copyright © Debbie Avery, 1982. All rights reserved. Reprinted by permission.

Paula Finn for "My father . . . " and "My dear father . . . ," by Paula Finn. Copyright © Paula Finn, 1983. All rights reserved. Reprinted by permission.

Jean E. Attebury for "My Father . . . ," by Jean E. Attebury. Copyright © Jean E. Attebury, 1983. All rights reserved. Reprinted by permission.

Linda DuPuy Moore for "When I was young," by Linda DuPuy Moore. Copyright © Linda DuPuy Moore, 1981. All rights reserved. Reprinted by permission.

Contemporary Books, Inc., for "Only a Dad," by Edgar A. Guest. From the book COLLECTED VERSE OF EDGAR A. GUEST. Copyright © Edgar A. Guest, 1934. And for "I think Daddy," by Loretta Lynn. From the book COAL MINER'S DAUGHTER, by Loretta Lynn. Copyright © Loretta Lynn, 1976. All rights reserved. Reprinted by permission.

Alfred A. Knopf, Inc., for "I am always," by Kahlil Gibran. From the book BELOVED PROPHET: The Love Letters of Kahlil Gibran and Mary Haskell, and Her Private Journal, by Kahlil Gibran and Mary Haskell. Edited and arranged by Virginia Hilu. Copyright © 1972 by Alfred A. Knopf, Inc. All rights reserved. Reprinted by permission.

Stephen Richard Tapogna for "To My Father," by Stephen Richard Tapogna. Copyright © Stephen Richard Tapogna, 1983. All rights reserved. Reprinted by permission.

Edith Schaffer Lederberg for "When Parents Become Friends . . . ," by Edith Schaffer Lederberg. Copyright © Edith Schaffer Lederberg, 1983. All rights reserved. Reprinted by permission.

Maureen Peake for "When you have the love," by Maureen Peake. Copyright © Maureen Peake, 1983. All rights reserved. Reprinted by permission.

Sue Mitchell for "Dad, why did it take me," by Sue Mitchell. Copyright © Sue Mitchell, 1983. All rights reserved. Reprinted by permission.